I'M HERE FOR THE HUMAN EXPERIENCE

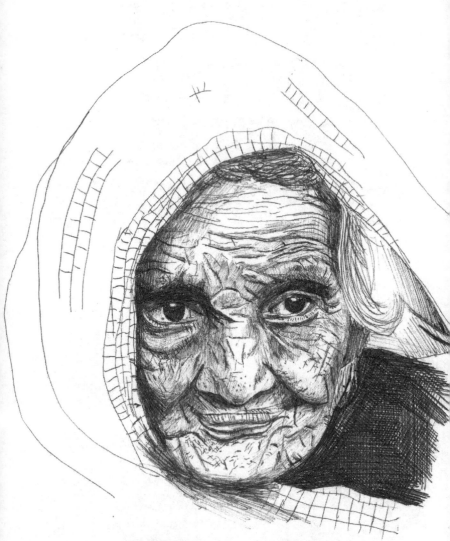

ME TOO

ME TOO

ME TOO

ME TOO

I'M NOT

Take Hair

Rob Auton
Illustrated by the Author

Burning Eye

This edition published by Burning Eye Books 2017
www.burningeye.co.uk

@burningeyebooks

Burning Eye Books
15 West Hill, Portishead, BS20 6LG

ISBN 978-1-911570-06-6

Also available by Rob Auton from Burning Eye:

In Heaven The Onions Make You Laugh
Petrol Honey

*Don't ever let fear turn you against
your playful heart*

Jim Carrey

A Letter From Father Christmas

Some of the most challenging sleeps I have ever had came as a child on Christmas Eve. I knew if I achieved sleep my reward would come in the shape of Father Christmas having been. This year I woke up to find I had received a letter from Father Christmas.

It read:

Dear Rob, I hope you have enjoyed the presents I have given you over the years, I have certainly got great pleasure from reading your lists. This year I thought I could give you my Christmas list. I realise you are busy and may not be able to meet all my requirements but I would really appreciate it if you could find the time to give it a go. I know you've got no way of checking, but I think I've been a good man this year. I have been a loving husband and have kept the reindeer in good health. Rudolph recently became a father, his son was not born with a red nose though so there is controversy surrounding the question of who the father is. Please find my Christmas list enclosed.

When I read that I thought 'You what? How dare Father Christmas send me his Christmas list? I don't know who is Father Christmas to Father Christmas but it is definitely not me. I am Father Christmas to nobody. Hold on a minute, if Father Christmas has sent me his Christmas list, does that mean Father Christmas believes in me? If someone believes in me I don't want to give them a reason not to.' I took the list and began to read it.

Rob, there is just one gift I would like from you this year. As a gift to me I would like you to attempt to become as comfortable within yourself when you are awake as you are when you are asleep.

Why have you become quieter and more withdrawn in social situations? Please don't disappear into yourself completely. It's acceptable to shut yourself off from the world when you are asleep but not when you are awake. Stop overthinking every single thought you have. Anxiety is not the capital of you. Take note of the words you wrote down that the cricket commentator said "Try your best, but don't take yourself too seriously." My elves have been watching you talk to yourself in your kitchen when you are on your own, they tell me what you say and I don't believe what you think of yourself is true. They told me that recently you said you prefer being asleep to being awake, that you feel like you fit in when you are asleep. I know you don't believe that.

Sleep is the cement that sticks your days together. Over time your days build up. From them create something you can be proud of. Yourself. When you fall asleep and do something in your dreams it doesn't stay. You can't work on any relationships in your sleep. There is no progress. You've got a recurring life that is in your hands when you wake up. Make the most of it. A recurring dad you can phone up. It's solid. Kate planted some sweet peas in the garden didn't she? Never in your wildest dreams will that happen. You are awake. Act like you are out of bed. Do something to make yourself tired while you still can. Grip your waking hours by the scruff of the minutes. Lie down on a night knowing you have earnt your horizontal time. Try to go to sleep looking forward to the absolute untameable mission that is tomorrow.

It is challenging being awake but worms do it, it can't be that hard. When did sleep become your happy place? You used to drive, now it's as if you are falling asleep at the wheel of your own life. Work to be brave, make your sleeping life the shadow of your waking life. The dream version of you will look on with envy watching you fight in the ring of reality you are attempting to carve out for yourself, because the other reality, that hashtag pray for reality isn't quite cutting it.

Go to bed knowing anything you achieve in your dreams isn't going to come close. You have never had your hair cut in your

11

dreams Rob, or had a shower, or shaved, or bought clothes. That guy is in a right state. All his teeth have fallen out. Not that he has ever looked in the mirror. He has never washed up or cleaned the bathroom. He has never opened an envelope with your name on it. He has never been to sleep. He must be absolutely knackered. He could fly but he doesn't. What does that mean? Maybe you are not bothered about flying? Public transport is there, may as well use it. The most memorable thing he has ever done is when he had the chocolate all the way through Kit Kat experience with an apple. He bit into it to find it was skin all the way through and continued to bite into it until it disappeared.

Sleep is the cocoon and I want you to wake up in the morning and break out of that sleep shell head first. Fly at it fuelled by your favourite cocktail, self-doubt and determination. The smell of ripening tomatoes. The sight of returning green cycle helmet through living room window. Walk. Pace. Run. Walk. Pace. Run. Get into them. Get broken and heal. I want the gulf between the awake and the asleep versions of you to widen. Attempting to instigate some sort of awakening within yourself every time your eyes open from a night sleep is too much to ask, I've tried it. This year Rob, I really want you to prove you are awake. I want you to do this for me as you've seemed so disconnected from everything and everyone of late. Being awake is other people, those you know and those you do not. If what some of them are doing makes you prefer the sleep side of your life, they have won. Do not allow them to win. Don't detach yourself from what you love. Plug yourself into the mains of what you have been born into and switch yourself on while you still have the chance. This isn't a present for me Rob, it is a present for you.

All the best,
Your friend and constant observer
Father Christmas

Entertainment

We'll treat it as entertainment shall we?

What shall we treat as entertainment?

That tree over there, the one with the sky behind it.

Yes OK. Has the entertainment started yet?

Yes it has.

We have missed the beginning haven't we?

Yes we have.

Will we miss the end?

Yes we will.
We have to make the most of the bits we get to see.
Catch them in our thought nets.
A quickly reversing car.
The colours of the junk mail on the doormat.
The sun shining on the last orange in the fruit bowl.
Barbecue smoke passing across the in bloom passion flower.
We are futuristic to those who are gone.
Historic to those who are to come.
We owe it to them to have a look at it all.

The Front Of My Face

I like faces
I like faces so much, I've got one
I've got one on the front of my head
If people see me and I see them
I introduce them to my face without saying anything
Faces have the power to bring things to life
Humans
Hoovers
Trains
If I was a train like Thomas the Tank Engine
My face would be the face on the front of the engine
My life is a train
A train with my face fixed to the front of it
Right now
My face is at the very front of my life
The tip of my nose is ever so slightly in the future
My past is carried behind me
The carriages of my train full of memories and faces
My old faces
Every expression is piled up
Smiles
Frowns
The ones in between and outside of them
Life is coming at me
I can feel it
A ski jumper mid-flight without goggles on
The motionless wind of time hitting me in the face
As I speed slowly into my future

Lifelines and Landlines

Is this what I feel like when I'm happy?
I'm enjoying pulling these weeds from the gravel
The sound design is faultless
Unseen understone breaking of roots
How could I be more content?
If the weeds weren't here with me?
Would that improve my mood?
I wouldn't think about the weeds if they were not here for me
to work on
I've got my brown suede slippers on
I only came down this shed end for a look
Now I've got a pile on the go
Grey dry dirt finger ends doing what they were meant for

It's Monday morning in October
I've just seen the frantic underbelly of a woodlouse
Resuscitated fossil
Full of levers and bars
Lead in colour
Should be stone but woodlice are made from themselves
and brilliance
Legs and arms without a need for feet or hands

What more do I need than this goalkeeper-free weed goal?
People applauding me for enjoying myself?
How could I feel more successful when pulling up a weed?
I could have a gardener doing it for me
He or she would find me when he or she has done it
Having achieved what I could have
My phone is in the house
Just like it was in my parent's garden
I love being outside with empty pockets
These weeds are landlines
And mental stability is ringing me on them

Good Boy

Our neighbours that we can hear have got a new puppy
I saw the boxes in the recycling
The lady says words to it such as

Good boy

and

No

I have started to pretend the lady is talking to me as a result of
my actions
Since I started writing this
I have been called a 'good boy' four times
It feels fantastic to be encouraged
Oh, she just shouted

NO

Maybe she didn't like that line about being encouraged
She is right, I must never ever get over confident
She is instructing me to sit but I am already sitting down
Oh, I'm a good boy again now
I must have sat down even more
Not sure how I pulled that off
We are back on track
When she asks the question
Who's a good boy then?
I say

Me
I am

Last night she repeatedly told me to leave
I'm not going anywhere
I don't know how I will feel if I see the puppy
I will probably feel ashamed that I have been using
compliments aimed at him for my own sake

Sometimes when the puppy is left alone
He makes high-pitched noises
Like a windscreen wiper
When nobody is calling him a good boy I want to shout

GOOD BOY

Just to make myself feel better if anything

Team Of Time

With the current level of conflicting beliefs and opinions
I am surprised people continue to agree on what time it is
What time is it?
6.40
Yeah I think that too
No it is, that is the right time
Why?
Because we say it is
Well it can be whatever time you want it to be
If you've got the guts
I thought watches would be set according to personal preference
People are working as a team whether they like it or not
I set my watch to the same time as everyone else
To make my life more manageable
To be in sync
To co-operate
To have yet another thing in common with someone I don't
know
A watch is a wristband to the festival of punctuality
We are all watching the same band
I can ask a stranger what the time is and believe in something
Time is a handrail to steady us through the dark and light
Hours differ around the globe but the minutes match
It is 41 past in Japan
No amount of sea, language or culture can put a minute
between us
Attempting to catch life as it barges past
The hands of time have a grip on its coattails
If it was just me here on Earth I don't know if I would bother
with time
I wouldn't need to know
Time is for when there is more than one person
How did word get around Britain that it was just gone twenty to
seven?
People say there are not enough hours in the day
Why don't we change it?
Put some more in?

What are we? Scared?
What do we think is going to happen?
All the people who said it was sixty minutes in an hour have
been dead for ages
I'm amazed gangsters and murderers subscribe to the same
times and numbers as me
It makes them seem a bit wet
They are not individual or powerful enough in spirit to set
their watches to a different time
If I set my watch to eleven hours and twenty three minutes
behind
Who is the real rebel now?
It's quarter past two in the afternoon by my watch but it's dark
outside, everyone is in bed and all the shops are shut

DOT TO DOT
FOR FANS OF
JACKSON POLLOCK

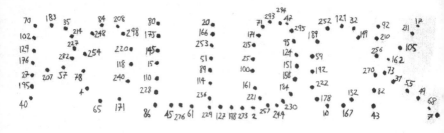

Sound Of Sandwich

Egg mayonnaise on white is the quietest sandwich I have heard
Teeth bite down into dry and wet silence
It's as if someone has told it off

Don't sulk
You are a sandwich
It could be worse

Sound insulation made from bread
Puts the mouth on mute
A vacuum of taste
Ideal cinema or library food
Quiet in volume
Deafening in smell

Nephew Colours

My nephew is at the Christmas tree
Tapping the baubles

What colour's that one Joseph?

He looks around and up at me and says

Orange

Wow, yes that's right

He has learnt what orange is since the last time I saw him
What have I done?

What about this one?

Blue

Says my dad
I look around at my dad and say

Yes

My dad smiles
He knows what colours are too
But he likes to keep his hand in
I point at one and say

Red

Grandson, grandad and uncle
United by colour and Christmas
For a few special moments

Water Again

What is water?
Water is the smell of a pint of orange cordial
Before you've added the cordial
Similar in taste to the broken pelvis of a melted snowman
The backbone of a snowflake
The unsalted tear of a poodle
The elbow of a puddle
The heartbeat of all wetness
Ground softener for the trowels
Purpose giver to the towels
Transporter of pills
Can't travel up hills
Spacious housing estate without walls for some lucky lucky
fish
Sometimes gives people a licence to throw a coin in and make
a wish
Mother nature's womb for the frog spawn
Wet film set for the frog's porn
WAR! TER!
Something for the ducks to have a little float on
Somewhere for a pirate to sail a little boat on
Water
Hype man for the bubble bath POP POP POP POP POP
Guaranteed to make the babies laugh
Bath time equals laugh time
When you're young
Not so much anymore for me
I have showers I don't have toys
Me standing still in the shower holding a yellow plastic duck
would just be sad now
When I was little I got put in the bath with my sister and my
cousins I don't know how
War! Ter!
Arch-enemy of the Dyson Airblade
Gave a home to a Disney mermaid
Ariel
Ariel mixed with water makes your clothes clean

If you've got a washing machine
Water
The driving force behind all damp and rust
If you paint a picture of the Earth from space include the blue bits yes you must
Transparent temperamental faceless monster that will take your life if you give it chance
On the other hand inspires quite creative things
Like the 1994 Eurovision Song Contest interval performance of the Riverdance
WAR! TER!
Playground for the dolphins
I saw the list of the top one hundred things to do before you die for dolphins
Swim with humans was not on it
Number one on the list was MEET FLIPPER
Water
The opposite of pastry
Soup for people who don't like ingredients, or soup
Oil rejector
Plant erector
Thirst corrector
Without water we'd be eating teabags
Would we?
What would a cup of tea be if water didn't exist?
A teabag in a mug
Would there be a teabag?
No
Would there be a mug?
No
Would there be a kettle?
No
Would there be a work surface?
No
Without water what would there be?
A need for water
I need water because I am alive. I know I'm alive due to the fact the self-service checkout in Sainsbury's asks me the question "Do you wish to continue?" What? Yes. Well… I thought I did,

until you asked me that. I imagine that question has triggered a few breakdowns in supermarkets. Do you wish to continue? Yes of course I do. That's the whole point of a supermarket. You go there if you wish to continue. If I didn't wish to continue I don't think I would be in a supermarket would I? I'd be at home, discontinuing myself off. Water allows me and all other living things to continue. Ducks. You don't see many ducks as roadkill. That's a positive. Why didn't the duck cross the road? It just didn't. Too busy having an alright time somewhere else. I wish I could float without trying. Do ducks even try? They seem so at ease with their own existence. They've got a peculiar perfection to them haven't they? Ducks. Rarely a feather out of place. Still only got one word in their entire vocabulary though. What if ducks learnt another word? What would it be? Sack? Quack sack. A duck is more than just a quack sack. Is it? I don't know. Water's massive for ducks, and me. Sometimes. Not always. Sometimes it's quite small. I've seen a drip and I've also seen a drop. I think I'd go as far to say that I have seen a drip drop and I've also seen a drop drip. Maybe the drop I saw was a drip. It's difficult to tell which ones are drops and which ones are drips. Does a drop need to get inside for it to become a drip? Why trouble myself with such questions? Is it a distraction? A distraction from what?

Brain Jazz

Standing on the floor under ground
She approached
All woolly hat and open mouth
A face with age for makeup
The back of her hand now faintly touching my waterproof
sleeve

Excuse me dear, may I leave my suitcase here with you?
I am going to walk up and down the platform
Get my circulation going

I agreed before thinking and found myself standing with a
silver plastic suitcase
Worried but pleased I looked trustworthy enough to look after
a suitcase
Is this what suspicious behaviour is?
Am I supposed to notice this?
It's difficult to recognise what you are supposed to notice
She walked full lengths of the platform
Smiling as she passed me and her case
With her circulation going again she came to a standstill

Thank you young man
I am getting the train
Where I live there is jazz festival
Have you heard of jazz?
Have you heard of jazz festival?

She looked away, with her ear facing me, waiting for me to
feed it something to hear

Yes I have heard of both

She looked at me and said
At jazz festival the children dance
What an inspiration, young children dancing
Have you heard of Cardiff?

Have you heard of Essex?

Yes I've heard of both Essex and Cardiff

Canary?
Have you heard of canary?
Bird?
Wow such flight
Have you heard of spider?
Different aren't they?
Webs and legs
Unfamiliar daily routine to me and you
Fire guards?
Earthquakes?
Apricots?
Strobe lighting?
Electric car?
So clever some people aren't they young man?
Have you heard of rain?
Really wet sometimes
Not always
Often just right

She made me think of parts of living I had heard of
and I appreciated it
As if life was a large meal and she was asking me which bits I
had tasted

People walked past unknowing of the pyrotechnics she was
putting on in my head
Lighting fuses to images with words I knew

Words Taken From A Press Conference And Put Into A Different Order To Make Myself Feel Better About What Was Being Said

I have to say one other thing
Look
Outside
Big
Big
So high
So nice
Very substantial colour
A billion scene
A world
A vital fortress
So strongly vulnerable
I think you care
of various stuff
Large and tremendous

Brilliant

I must point out
Number one
I saw other people
Outstanding in every case
I strongly believe in incredible things

Minds
Effort
Beautiful intelligence
We must defend extreme common sense
Life
Truly
The biggest story in the history of stories

Evolved For Tuesday

As a human I am evolved to the point of working to a deadline
And lying awake at night worrying about it
I narrowly missed out on sitting on a warm shed roof on a
Tuesday afternoon licking myself clean
I also missed out on not knowing what Tuesday afternoon is
What's so bad about knowing what Tuesday afternoon is?
Tuesday afternoons
They're alright
Not that I can remember many
At the time of writing I cannot remember any
When I watch an action film I never think of the action being
filmed on a weekday
Some of 'Star Wars' was almost definitely filmed on a Tuesday
afternoon
Adults dressed up in costumes as children are busy at school
Would I be more content if I didn't know the meaning of
Tuesday?
What is the meaning of Tuesday?
Depends I guess
Maybe if I made up my own word for Tuesday
Instead of living by what others have set up?
I'm a slither away from a biro being a mystery to me
I almost didn't need to write anything down
Sometimes when people ride their bikes on the pavement
I wish I had missed out on evolution
Put me in a pond where I cannot get cycled on
If I had fins I wouldn't need to know where to find my HMRC
login number
But I want to embrace the comfort of corduroy trousers
Scrubbing the pan after overcooked scrambled eggs
Eventually scraping with a spoon
On a Tuesday afternoon

Surprise Sticker

Once again I find myself dog-earing a corner on purpose
To see if it is a sticker or not
Head arched over
Chin touching my chest
Is this one of them?
The investigation consumes me
Until I arrive at a definite conclusion
It is normally the difference in the two sides
That has got me thumbing with a frown
I check because once when I was younger
I didn't think something was going to be a sticker
and it was
I remember the first time I experienced the surprise
Of adhesive in disguise
One becoming two like that
Such undisturbed freshness
It made me think to question things more
Find out what they really are
I don't check everything to see if it is a sticker or not
Like a sniffer dog I can recognise a potential result
When something warrants exploration
I do my best to pull it apart

Potato Heat

I was boiling new potatoes again
A canvas for seasoning
In the sieve they dried themselves off with their hot insides
Just like humans do but quicker
If steam was their voice
These potatoes were miming opera

On wet, just washed, thin lime green chopping board
I attempted to hold the heat in place with my fingerprints
Cutting the potatoes in half to fry and get some much needed
tonight crispy bits
I went to put one of my hot holding fingers in my eye
I presume it was to itch it
With my finger in my eye
I remembered my finger was hot and in my eye
It felt gorgeous
I had never had a hot eye before
It felt correct to me
Made me wonder if I would feel more relaxed if I had hot eyes
Instead of whatever temperature they are at normally
Eyes are kept at headroom temperature

The boiling water had made the potato hot
My finger hot
and then it had made my eye hot

Sometimes unorganised events like this happen to me
and I am pleased to be here
Here where potato coals grow in the cold ground and end up
warming the eyes of the tired

Documentme

If I saw myself on screen in a nature documentary
I would get to find out what it is that I am doing
The voice-over letting me in on my own behaviour
Why I'm driven to do what I do

Here we see an adult male standing up on a stage
He is reading out an idea he has had
Having written the idea down in private
He is now compelled to share it with an audience
He is doing this because

Yes?
Go on tell me please
This should be interesting

Because he is in a constant state of attempting to prove to himself
that he is alive in his body. He is afraid of leaving without
having tried his best to convey how he feels about the place he
has found himself on. Growing older he has begun to focus on
his temporary state. Aware that he will only get to know what
shampoo is once. That sunsets are going to take place whether
he is alive to see them or not. How unlikely it is that he gets
to talk about sheep. He wants to minimize isolation in the all-
encompassing word that is universe. To ask others what answers
they have for this questionless exam.

Is it? Is that the reason?
Dissect my actions like you do for the bottle nose dolphins off
the coast of Florida
Trapping the fish in their homemade mud rings
I need to know
Tell me what I must do to understand myself

In a state of almost constant agitation
He often fails to see what the meaning of it is
He is comforted by his battle
I think

Shopping For Sexes

Leave the cauliflower
Don't worry about her

The lady with the trolley and the child has made her mind up
Cauliflowers are female
Her words drip with unforgiving supermarket fact
For a moment I am transported to a place where vegetables
and fruit have gender
I try to think of some for myself but they seem predictable and
done
Peaches, bananas, satsumas
I want to explore her gift
Ask her what other pieces of the world are
Is concrete a he or a she?
Not masculine or feminine
I want to know what toilet concrete uses
How would it feel to walk down a street where windows and
doors are men and women?
It made me appreciate the simplicity of the sexless
Bins
Guttering
Bulldog clips
The backs of chairs

WHAT'S HONEY?

This And That

How am I supposed to come to terms with this?
When it is other people who are telling me what this is
Welcome to this
Look at this
We call this this
This goes here
If we do this
This will happen
Sometimes when we say this
This doesn't happen
We are fine with this
We know this has happened before
So this is what we continue to do
You know this
They know this
You want this
They want this
Everyone wants this
Let me tell you about this
Have you seen this?
Watch this
Have you heard this?
Listen to this
Have you tasted this?
Have you smelt this?
Have you felt this?
You need to do this to get this
This is not what bad looks like
This is what good looks like
This is what it's all about
This is the future
This is the next big thing
If you look like this and sound like this you will get this
We are all for this

What about that?

No ignore that
You don't want that
You want this
Not that

I don't like this
I don't agree with what this stands for
This doesn't add up
This doesn't seem to be working
This is broken
I'm not comfortable with this
Maybe it's time for us to give that a go

Take no notice of that
Why do you want that when you can have this?
Look at this
Look at all of this
Look how much of this there is
There is so much of this
How can this be wrong when there is so little of that?

That looks like it might be better for everyone
That looks peaceful, compassionate, human
That looks like it might have empathy
I'm going to take a bit of this and I'm going to go over there
and make it that

No

Yes
I'm going to turn that into this

That's not yours

This is mine now

Birds For Leaves

East London pavement trees
Silently consenting into pins for posters
Unasked for acupuncture
How many lost cats have found themselves back in the warmth
thanks to these forest representatives?
Neck models for last season's bike lock jewellery
Voluntary territory markers
Spelling out the seasons for us like pound shops
Growing their temporary decorations
Same ones as last year if I remember correctly
Leaves
Badly expressed humming birds reversed out from the branches
Stem beaks sucking at their place of birth
Filling themselves with the nature of city life

Balding

On the train to Brighton we speak of hairs departing the aging
station of my head
Intercity Vo5s dropping out of my life
Gently falling to their various destinations

You'll be like Alain de Botton, she said

Why what does he do? I replied

He's a philosopher

No, with his hair

Simple

I am simple
Simple as something that will drip if you pierce it
Simple as something that will wither if you don't water it
Simple as something that will freeze if you cool it

My brain doesn't agree with me
Tells me I'm complicated
Complicated as something I can't understand

I wish my mind was in charge of my thoughts
To keep myself away from where they take me
To keep myself simple

MY BODY KEEPS ME ALIVE, OR IS IT THE OTHER WAY AROUND?

Intimidation Techniques Of A Robin

Standing on the small strip of garden having carried out some light maintenance, a robin landed a metre away on the recently disturbed mud that we rent. I thought I knew what robins did. I believed I had seen the behaviour of robins enough to predict how the next few moments would unfold. I would move towards the robin, the robin would look at me, be still for a blink, and then fly off. Leaving me with the feelings I get when I have just seen a robin. The opposite of annoyed. Pleased to have seen a bit of free colour. I looked at all the parts that came together to build the robin and thought, go on then, do what you normally do. You've given me the correct amount of time that robins allocate to humans. Without fail you leave us wanting more. Let's keep it as it's always been. Our lives are too different for us to form a solid friendship. Instead of flying away, the robin took a step towards me. Not a sequence of steps. One properly pronounced step. Really lifting that foot off the ground, moving it forward for a semi-circle before returning it to the ground. Sometimes when one step is taken instead of several, I find the step becomes more dramatic. As if someone is really thinking about what they are going to do and more to the point, if they should be doing it. I didn't expect this from a robin, and I am not saying a robin is a someone. "Should I be doing this?" is not what I hear going through a robin's head. I began my lowering to the ground manoeuvre, starting at the knees, keeping my back straight, not breathing too much. The robin was still still. My knees had got me as low as they could. I had never seen a bird so secure in its own feathers as that robin. Turning its head, I could see one of its eyes. Too much eyes for a bird that size. Those eyes must be heavy in the head. Unlike mine. I can't feel the weight of my eyes. Are eyes the heaviest component of a robin? Black all the way through. I had been looking at the eye for long enough for us to have entered into a staring contest but the competitive element was nowhere to be seen. The robin blinked. So quietly. I had never seen a robin blink before. Where did all that eyelid come from? Must have a good hiding place for that. No eyelashes though. When I see a robin I always think of it to be a man but it occurred to me that this was a woman. She had motherly, sisterly and daughterly qualities to her. How fragile do you have to be before you start needing a robin to tell you everything is going to be alright? She continued to advance towards me, keeping eye contact and there was no way, NO WAY, that I was going to back away from the ancestor of a small Christmas dinosaur. I knelt, she stood. She couldn't kneel. You need knees to do that and robins were busy when knees were being issued. Do birds have a bad posture? Get your shoulders back. What was this situation I had found myself in on a Saturday afternoon? I thought my eyesight had been getting worse recently but the robin was as in focus as frogs are on the adverts for HD televisions. She was plugged in and switched on and I was getting a really good episode of this robin's soap opera. A bird so friendly and familiar I wanted to ask her if we had met before. "Sorry, do I know you?" I didn't. I could see the small shine of the claws. The tiny rings of skin around the legs. I creased my nose up so my top lip lifted slightly, and moved my eyebrows down as if trying to bring my nose and eyebrows together. Crouched down I laughed in the robin's direction as if we had shared a joke. The bird looked at me remembering what she was and flew away. Just when you start to believe you have got a few things figured out, a tame robin comes and turns your brain on its head by coming a bit too close for a bit too long.

Ticket For The Sunset

A Travelodge sits in the audience for the Dorset sunset
The light show colouring the white walls pink
That pink with the orange blood
The building relaxes in the row behind the water
Boats watch from the lap of their wet parent
Distracted
As if they are too young to understand it
I like it today
Gravity
Breath
Body
The way my fingers end
My blood stops
and it's not me anymore
Every now and then the sky makes sense again
Puts its fingers in my ears and gives me some quiet time

We are now approaching

The hushed cowgirl hatted hen do leaves the carriage
My rucksack sits on the seat next to me
A new to the train man is now sitting on my rucksack

Can I go twos on a rolly mate?

His girlfriend is laughing into half a jet pack sized cider bottle

I'm sorry I don't smoke

He collapses onto the seat next to her and laughs into her neck
Other people change it
For better and for worse
It's dark now and the train lights are on

Hygiene

Her name is Gene
She likes being clean
When people see her they say

Hi Gene

And she says

Yes it is very important

Bradford Hotel Weekday Morning

A male member of staff is filling up black tapped clear Perspex
juice dispensers
Nothing is going through his head that isn't getting said

We're getting there now

He looks at the juice colours and nods
He looks at the people and nods
Gives them eye contact but doesn't get it back

We're getting there now

It becomes apparent he has a stop start mantra

We're getting there now

Recently asleep people awakewalk
Onto the warm serve yourself buffet pitch
It is clear from the faces, the novelty of all you can eat has lost
its heat for some

On televisions
On walls
On mute
With subtitles on

We're getting there now

His words ricochet off the ears of fellow staff members onto the
floor

We're getting there now

Where are we going?
Fork touches triangular raised bed of first hash brown
My favourite area in the circular garden of cooked breakfast

We're getting there now

Where? The end of my hash brown
Food turns future into past fast
The sun goes in
It doesn't go out
He tips new bacon to where people can get to it

We're getting there now

I know we are
I can feel it
My front bottom teeth aren't what they used to be
As I return for what I don't need he looks at me then to the
darkest cube of liquid and quickly back to me

Look we've got this new juice. Forest Fruits. Nobody's drinking
it. Will have to get a new sign up for this juice. Nobody's
drinking it. Forest Fruits. Good name for juice. Makes me think
about forests and fruits. Taste it, it's nice. Better than orange juice
every morning. Here you go. I've got four boxes of the stuff.
Still on my first box. Forest Fruits. Good name isn't it. Not
Forest Juice. FOREST FRUITS. Nobody's drinking it. I'm going
to have to put a sign up. A sign that says FOREST FRUITS. Get
them drinking it.

His supervisor appears
They speak
Some people breathe out and do what people do with
newspapers when they are annoyed
Nobody is saying we are getting there now anymore
I look at the people
It's as if they don't want to get to the same place as him

Wherever it is

We're getting there now

Sparrows And Mortar

House sparrows cling to the rented wall
The birds are eating the house
The landlord told me they eat the mortar
It helps them with their digestion

Even the sparrows know what they are doing
What is wrong with me?

The sparrows figured it out for themselves
I guess that is what I am trying to do
I know there is a wall for me to cling to somewhere
To help me with the task of digesting my own life

Crown

Field in a countryside
Wearing a crown
It doesn't sit right
Fields don't need royalty
They are fields
Not kings and queens

Sheep in a field
Wearing a crown
It doesn't sit right
Sheep don't need royalty
They are sheep
Not kings and queens

Tree in a forest
Wearing a crown
It doesn't sit right
Trees don't need royalty
They are trees
Not kings and queens

Crow in a nest
Wearing a crown
It doesn't sit right
Crows don't need royalty
They are crows
Not kings and queens

Human in a building
Wearing a crown
It doesn't sit right
Humans don't need royalty
They are humans
Not kings and queens

Heat Return

A girl so selfless
She will wear a jumper
To keep the jumper warm
Speaks under her breath into raised cuff
Like bodyguard behind president

Are you warm enough?
Are you sure?
Let me know if you need me to exercise won't you?
By the way
Thanks for everything

Once she has warmed the jumper up
The jumper goes to work on her
Elbows and shoulders on the receiving end of karma
Feeling it relaxing upon her upper body hinges
Her warmth is returned to its place of birth

Covered In Sleep

I like sleeping. How do you feel about sleeping? Do you enjoy having a break from yourself? I know I do. If being awake is a journey, I am a nervous passenger. I surrender to sleep every night. My duvet is my chubby white flag. I went to sleep last night. Not that I had much of a choice in the matter. It's difficult to shake off the habit of a lifetime. I'm going back to sleep tonight. No you can't look at it like that. Life is not one big sleep with inconvenient daily interruptions of being awake. I had a really good night last night. Did you? What did you do? I went to sleep. Have you done it? Wow. It was as if I wasn't bothered about anything. I'm doing it again tonight I don't care anymore, I've had an awakening.

I'm typing this as the awake version of myself, the asleep version of me isn't here, he's in bed. Well he will be… when I get there. I'm not saying I sleep with myself. I guess I am. When you sleep with yourself you are sleeping with a member of your own family. Does that make me inbed?

I have been trying to explore sleep but it's difficult to explore sleep when you are awake. I attempted to carry out sleep research when I was asleep, but I got too close to the subject. I am excited that we've all been to sleep and we will be going to sleep again. Sometimes I look at people in the street and think "I know what you've been doing." I am excited by that but I am not excited by the fact that some of us walk around like we've got absolutely nothing in common.

Hiya

Sorry do I know you?

Well you don't know me no but I wake up on a morning and I go to sleep on a night and in between I just do the best I can to keep myself alive. You don't know the finer details but we are pretty much the same.

That was a conversation between me and a pigeon.

Even though I do it on a regular basis sleep is not something that I can be particularly passionate about. It's part of me and my life that I have to accept, think nothing of and be bored by, like my skeleton, my throat and my earlobes. Sleep is built into me. Included in the popular package deal I have subscribed to since birth called 'life'.

When they were designing sleep they must have said "This stuff has to exist. It's important that we give them some time away from it all and each other. There's going to be a mass amount of information for them to attempt to digest when they are awake. To be honest it will be a miracle if people are not fainting due to the fact they have a tongue. We need them to sleep. They can't just be awake all the time, that won't work. If people are awake all the time how is anyone going to know when to have breakfast?"

All my family sleep. My (fictional) uncle is the loudest snorer. One night when he was asleep the wind changed direction and it swapped round. So now when he's awake he snores to people instead of talking and when he's asleep he makes racist comments. I wouldn't say I'm a sleep fanatic. I don't have framed posters of sleep on my bedroom wall or anything like that, but I've got a bed. A bed isn't a poster is it? Well it can be. Bed is the only piece of furniture I go to. I'm going to bed. I have never been to chair. I'm going to table now. Pardon?
Table time come on.
You what?
It's your table time.
No it isn't.
Yes it is.
It's tea time. T.A.B.L.E time
No. The t in tea time does not stand for table.
Maybe we don't spend long enough on the sofa for us to say "I'm going to sofa."
You need to spend a lot of time on a piece of furniture for it to become a destination.
Yes I go to the toilet but I'm sorry I don't class a toilet as a piece of furniture.
If I were to view an unfurnished flat I would expect it to have a toilet.

Sorry, we really like this flat but there's one problem, we can't find the toilet.

Oh no this flat's unfurnished.

Unfurnished? It hasn't got a toilet. Unfinished is what it is.

Sometimes different parts of my body go to sleep before I'm ready for bed. If it's my hand I say "No not yet please. We can't do it here I'm not ready. Are you trying to go to sleep without me? You can go to sleep but you will never have a dream without me."

One time recently I was in bed and I woke up because my hand had gone to sleep. I said "Excuse me, what are you doing? We aren't taking it in turns. I was doing it for all of us. We've got to stick together. You can't go off on your own. We are a unit. You think you can be twice as asleep as me?"

We were all in bed last night weren't we? Big sleepover on Earth last night. Massive. Very well attended. Me, you, all our relatives, dogs, cats, herons, Michael Burke, Pauline Quirke, Ian Brown in sleepy town. Enya. Enya with her eyes shut, the definition of peace and tranquillity. If I have a little girl I will call her Enya and I will look forward to saying "Enya's in bed, she's asleep."

Sleep is an international event, they were doing it in Italy last night. An Italian sleepover? Sounds classy. I bet there were candles. When I go to a foreign country and see that one of their customs is sleeping I think I'm going to fit in. It doesn't matter where I am, I feel at home when I'm asleep. At home in my own skin. I don't have to worry about what people think of me. I know what they think of me. They think I'm asleep. Society expects it of me. Sleep is a given. Freedom for the tired.

Sleepovers all over, tickets are free if you've got a body. The dress-code is the casual end of the 'smart casual' spectrum. It's still going on somewhere. Earth is the perfect venue for a sleepover. Thank you gravity. Did anyone else fall asleep in that film?

I live in a multicultural part of the world, Leyton in London, we all sleep. Different religions shedding their layers on a night. Agreeing on "I'm tired." We've got a spider staying with us in our flat at the moment. She sleeps on a web. The ghost of a hammock. When she moved in I said "I don't mind you staying with us but you're not going to crawl into my mouth when I'm asleep are you?" and she said "No Rob, it's not true that the average person swallows eight spiders a year when they are asleep, there is just one guy swallowing loads and loads of spiders on purpose and he gets the average up for everyone."

When shall we sleep? When it's dark yes? When the lights are off in Argos. Animals are you up for this? Cows? Nighttime sleeping? We are on the same page aren't we? Big eyed cows in barns calling it a day. What else are you meant to call it? Do cows think about tomorrow? Has a cow in the history of cows ever had an early night on purpose? "Big day tomorrow." Are all days the same size for cows? I can imagine a sleepy cow, the mouth, the buckling of knees, but some creatures seem far too awake to go to sleep. As far as I'm concerned, every squirrel I have ever seen could not have been more out of bed. Looking at me like that as if to say "I am a well-rested organism, I have improved memory and mood." I don't know what position squirrels sleep in. I like to think of them on their backs with their hands up. Squirrels look to be a long way from yawning.
If I saw a squirrel yawn, I believe it would force me to do the same. I respect them for their focus and work ethic. Yawning is the closest function I've got to a refresh button. You can't fake an authentic yawn. All these creatures yawning and sleeping having a nice nighttime sleep together. Makes me feel like I'm part of something. The alive gang. Owls? Hey? What do you think you're doing? The pigeons were in bed ages ago, they know when it's bedtime. You don't see pigeons sleeping during the day do you? A pigeon having a duvet day? It's not going to happen. I guess every day's a duvet day when you've got feathers like that. Come on. All living things having a nice big sleep together. We are meant to be in sync. You're messing it up. Oh badgers, get on board will you? We sleep together, we wake together. If dogs were nocturnal do you think they would

hold the title of 'Man's Best Friend'? Don't think so. A shared sleeping pattern has enabled relationships to blossom. You could have been dogs to us badgers. I just want to see badgers in the sunshine. To see what they look like with the sun on their fur. The shadow of a badger. Like the birds outside my house. They don't press snooze they don't have a snooze to press. They wake up and they are singing. Another day in paradise. They could lie in all day but they don't. What have birds got to get up for? Same as us. The world. We need them to get up. If birds didn't get up because they couldn't see the point in any of it what kind of an example would that be? I think birds set a fantastic example. They look intent on making the most of their time here. Leaving the nest, giving us something to look up to. It must be invigorating to fly out of bed on a morning. When a bird wakes up how long does it take it to remember it can fly? Probably the same amount of time it takes me to remember that I can't. Having sleep in common with elephants and blue tits helps me take people in high-powered jobs less seriously. "You're president of America. What did you do last night? Went to sleep? LIKE A PIG."

How do humans get to sleep? They count sheep.

How do sheep get to sleep? They count humans approaching them with knives and then they sleep forever.

SURELY WE SHOULD CONSIDER OURSELVES TO BE AS SPECIAL NOW

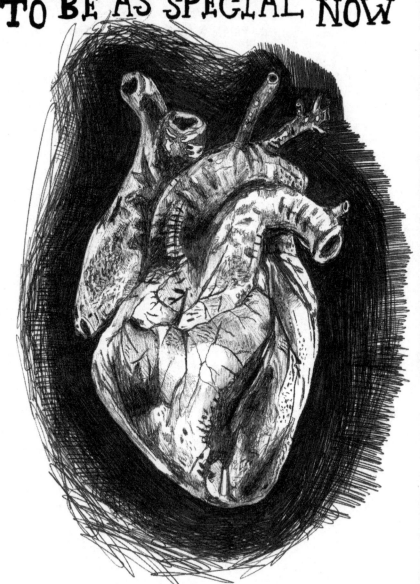

AS WE WERE WHEN WE WERE FIRST BORN

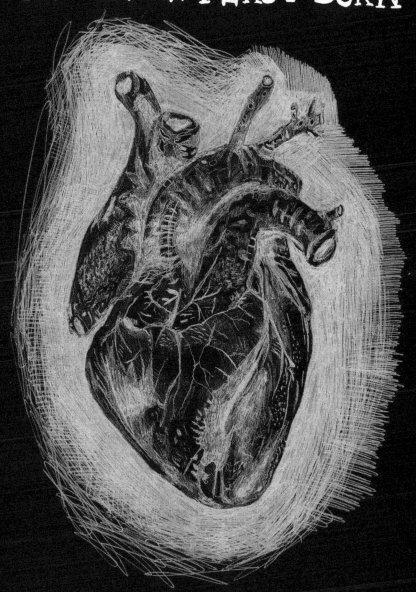

Hot Water Bottle Decision

Are we having a hot water bottle tonight?

Yes put the kettle on

One of my favourite answers
To one of my favourite questions
If I didn't have anyone to ask
I would ask myself

Am I having a hot water bottle tonight?

Yes put the kettle on

I met a lady recently who said she had two hot water bottles
One for the bedroom and one for the living room
What a luxury
Doesn't she know they are portable?
What was she? A millionaire?
Two hot water bottles?
What's the limit?
Eight
Imagine how warm that would be
How many hot water bottles can you have in a bed before it
becomes a waterbed?
If you fill a waterbed up with spring water is it better for your
back?
Electric blanket?
There's inventions to heat the bed up but what about cooling it
down?
Cold water bottles never really took off did they?
Well they did, outside of the bed
Get a bottle of water out of the fridge and put it in your bed?
No point
You'd just have a bottle of water in your bed

Somewhere To Sit

Take a seat
There wasn't a seat
So I sat down on the world
It felt like a huge achievement to sit on a planet
Still does
I got on
Hello
The Earth is breaking my fall
Preventing rainbows from being full circles
Jumping up and down on it on purpose
This place seems sturdy
How does movement of such a wild nature feel so still?
I thought there would be more turbulence
This can't be what it feels like to be on a spinning floating planet
People are bored
Is it finding rotations more of a challenge with this load?
Has this home to so much gained weight since the increase in
human population?
The dinosaurs weighed a lot, we are far lighter than they were
There are fewer elephants than before and we are burning trees
Perhaps the Earth is losing weight?
Furiously feeding on fossil fuels forces our firm home to become
polystyrene light
Light to the point of floating out of position
Walking home from Asda the bags were full of gravity and tins of
coconut milk
If the planet was put on the scales the tins would contribute to the
total weight
I will consume them in a Thai green curry and burn off the energy
Like nothing happened
What about all of this concrete?
The concrete was here already, just in different parts
It's bits of nature mixed up, like everything else
You can't live your life wondering if you are making the world
put weight on

Heart Mane

On occasion my heart swiftly sprouts the mane of a lion
Matted hairs of cadmium red and alizarin crimson
A featureless beating skull of glistening muscle and tube
I am demoted to position of body around it
The gangly vegetable patch surrounding the prize
The uncertain pool around the swimmer
Gasping for a personal best
Drags the rest of me forward without my brains consent
Forces me to believe in the facts of myself
The facts that I have laid
My foundations
Where I can stand my ground and say

Yes

Prawn Firm

My friend described prawns as firm
The perfect word for prawns
Sometimes words and images lock on
Prawn
Fits over what it is naming like a thin protective shell
Firm prawn
Between the fingers
Between the teeth
Full of themselves
Prawn shaped grape type creature
I am far from firm
Bones force me to feel breakable
If I was meat all the way through
Steady seedless prawn style
Maybe I would be less sensitive
Take more risks
Who has more to lose?
Me or a prawn?
It's about equal

Camouflage

I saw an elderly lady on the brink of Zimmer frame
Wearing a camouflage jacket and trousers
If her posture was a letter
It would have been a lowercase r
Her combat clothing, far from shades of green and brown
But bright heavy tessellating mappy patches
Gold
Silver
Rubies
Diamonds
Beauty encrusted metal
Beaming armour
When the sun hit her she exploded into her own
I want to see the landscape
Where you blend into the background in camouflage like that
What kind of battle was she fighting?
Where was it being held?
A war field of such immense colour and shine
People protected by the armour of beauty

Sky Museum

I paid a visit to the sky museum
On the walls were photographs
Skies of all ages
All ages post the invention of the camera
There was a large window if you wanted to look at the most
up-to-date sky
Surprisingly, looking out of the window was by far the biggest
attraction at the museum
Mona Lisa levels of lookers
Staring through the glass at the unpainted big stuff
Making comments such as

That sky is brand new. Look, we are the first people ever to get
to see that one. Can you take a photo of me and the latest sky?
Oh it's changed again, would you mind taking another one of
me with this new one?

To be honest I was surprised the museum had a roof
A large painting with nimbostratus clouds hung on the wall
A description read:
THIS IS WHAT SCIENTISTS BELIEVE PREHISTORIC SKIES
TO HAVE LOOKED LIKE
It looked overcast to me
To say it was a museum there was a distinct lack of authentic
pieces of antique sky to look at
They hadn't preserved any sky for the paying public to get
near
No waxworks or scale models like in the Jorvik Viking Centre
That's what I want from a museum
To get near something that I haven't been near before
I guess it's easier to dig things up than it is to pull them down

When To Live

I am often advised to live in the moment
Which moment?
Narrow it down for me
Show me the moment I am supposed to live in
This one?
Alright

Did it

Now what?
Wait for the next moment?
That's now
I just lived a moment ago
I've got to do it again?
I can't keep that up
Here's another one for you
Make sure you live in it
I can't find the tin opener
Embrace your inability to find the tin opener
Live in the moment of your bad memory and the unopened tin
Finding the tin opener is not a moment I want to live in
Some moments have better living conditions than others

I tell you what I'll do
I'll exist in the moment to give myself a chance of living in the
moment
That's the best I can do
You don't have to put your life into every moment
If you lived every moment you'd be shattered
Leave some moments empty
Don't put your life into moments that don't deserve it
Sometimes it is acceptable to exist in the moment

Cleaning your teeth
Putting your phone on charge
Stubbing your toe
Inserting a USB stick the wrong way round

Existing is underrated

You can't live if you don't exist
The moments that are worth living in creep up on me
When they do I try not to think about the moment
I don't want the moment to become a memory too quickly
Memories of moments are the ones I remember

Wild Air

Masses of furniture covered in air
Most of furniture
I've got some of it in my flat
Furniture with air all over it
Wild air settling down
Giving the pushy wind a wide berth
Relaxing
Taking the weight off
Filling up the empty bath like water in an ice cube tray
A welcome squatter of all shapes and sizes
Unique areas of air making itself at home
The air in the vasectomied fireplace of the bedroom
The only place in the world where that particular area of air is
It sits lightly on the cushions
Flops on the bed
Look at it
On your shoulders
Baguettes of air lagging around your arm pipes
Up my nose it goes for a brief taste of lung captivity
Selflessly giving me the present I need
Before its release through my mouth exit

Flight Stimulator

After the shortest of deliberation processes
I saw a pigeon make the decision to fly
A forward motion starting at the claws
Gripping into the pavement
The red of the lifting ankle
Folding into purple and back
Short hidden leg muscles doing their jobs
With an eye on each side of your head
I guess there is no need to look both ways
Instantly busy wings
No runway or clearance required
I have never seen two birds crash into each other
The air traffic controller for birds is thorough

Flight

I would like to see pigeons having to do a run up to take off
As helmet wearing humans do
When they try to fly in competitions
Running and flapping along a sunny jetty
Not knowing if their design is going to keep them out of the
water
Birds must feel superior when watching such contests
Pigeons don't need to work on their wings
They are passengers on board the vehicles of themselves

My Favourite Bakery

I wish I had a favourite bakery
I could buy people bread as a gift
As I hand it to them I would say

This is from my favourite bakery

Holding it with both hands
They would look into the brown paper bag and think

Rob is a man with a favourite bakery, I didn't realise he was
doing so well

Do I have a favourite bakery?
No
Why not?
I haven't put the effort in
What haven't I put the effort into?
I haven't put the effort into finding a favourite bakery
If I had, people would query where I found the time

How many times has he been there to have made it his
favourite? Not only that but how many other bakeries does he
know of that aren't his favourite? When did Rob become the
type of person who has a favourite bakery?

They would picture the new me opening the heavily
condensated door on a crisp Saturday morning
Gripping the worn gold-plated door handle with a brown
leather gloved hand
The bell ringing above the interior conversations
Inhaling through my nose with my eyes shut
Shaking my head when my lungs reach capacity
Opening my eyes to a familiar smile from behind the loaf-laden
counter

I would like to give someone supermarket bread as a
Christmas present
A wrapped up loaf of white sliced under the Christmas tree
would certainly have the shape of something worth opening
They would feel through the paper and think
It feels like bread but it must be clothes

THE FULL STOP IS MORE POWERFUL, THAN THE QUESTION MARK.

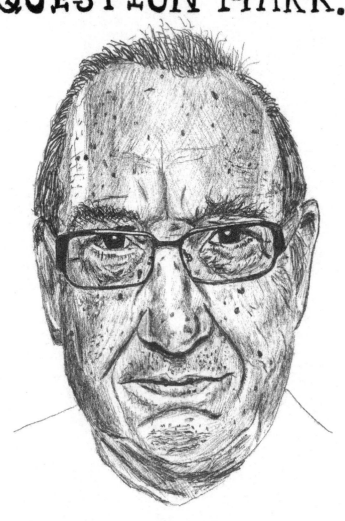

IS IT?

Fireworked

A firework froze at its climax
Exploded into a monument to itself
In the bright of the morning
Birds perched on its hovering colours
Blackbirds
Magpies
Pigeons
Starlings
Crows
Jays
Wrens
Blue tits on green bits
One bird per spark
Giving the firework a daytime existence
A feathered display
If the birdlife hadn't landed there
The firework may have gone unnoticed
Until the return of its preferred background
How cluttered our close sky would be
If fireworks burst and remained
Certain sights of the country under a forest canopy of light

Edinburgh Castle

We could look up to memories
The sky a display of captured excitement

Our Friend Who Does Magic

Ian is a magician
He likes to be called Magic Ian
But in one word
So we call him
Magician

Water Body

By weight, the average human adult is approximately
sixty-five percent water
I don't mind people telling me I'm wet
I am
I've got wet blood
I am soaking on the inside
I hope I am more than just a shape full of polluted water
With bits in it such as my heart
If I am sixty-five percent water
That means I am thirty-five percent me
and sixty-five percent water
Perhaps I am the cordial of me and the water in me makes me
less concentrated and able to swallow my own existence
If I feel like this, what must life be like for a cucumber?
By weight the average adult cucumber is approximately
ninety-six percent water
According to the NHS website a five centimetre piece of
cucumber counts as one of your five a day
In that case a glass of water is ninety-six percent of one of your
five a day
Why not put a handful of ice cubes on your salad
Take them to work in your lunch box
It doesn't matter if they melt
Just pour the remainder of the contents of your lunch box into
your mouth like a practically empty packet of crisps
If a cucumber is ninety-six percent water, does that mean water
is ninety-six percent cucumber?
Basically I am not far away from having cucumber for blood,
and they want me to start thinking about inheritance tax?
What's your National Insurance number?
Please enter the name of a memorable restaurant so you can
see how much your phone bill has gone up by
Do you wish to continue?
I do but I'm sorry if I find it quite difficult sometimes because
over half of me is a puddle that is just doing the best it can to
keep standing up

I have a mass amount of respect for the four percent that make
cucumbers cucumbers
Those four percents are putting a serious shift in
The fab four of fruit and veg
Two girls and two boys I think
Like Abba
Working around the clock to give cucumbers an identity of
their own
One percent is in charge of taste
One percent is in charge of shape
One percent is in charge of vitamin content
And the final one is in charge of colour
Multi-tasking for the creation of inner and outer green
It's busy
No wonder cucumber and tuna go so well together in
sandwiches
The tuna is close to being alive and back in the water
but instead it's dead and in bread
Sometimes I feel like I'm in a sandwich
Birth is the bottom slice of bread
Death is the top slice of bread and my life is the filling
On my deathbed for my final meal
I will be served the sandwich of my life
I want to be able to eat that sandwich
Safe in the knowledge I made the best sandwich I could
With the ingredients I had available to me
Ready
Steady
Live

Fridge Food Floor

Sunday afternoon
Cleaning out the fridge
The appliance is now at room temperature
If a kitchen is a room
A kitchen seems too functional to be a room
This kitchen is certainly not a function room
Still cold glass jars stand on wooden floor
Spread out in the style of partially knocked down bowling pins
Gherkins with a look from the lab
Marmalade icing the cake of itself with snow mould
Elderly mayonnaise Dijon mustarding at the edges

This was new once
This food
This fridge
This floor
Spinach leaves moved to liquid
Too cool to remain loyal to their shape
Squirty cream toxic at the nozzle
As if a Batman baddy has been tampering with it

I cut my knuckle trying to get a shelf back in
Tense clean again ageing plastic
Not as transparent as it once was
Hurting me for cleaning it
Swearing at the fridge on my own
This is a long way from bowling
What is a strike in this situation?
A clean fridge
I will not turn around to my friends and put my arms up
I know what's going to happen
The need to clean will return like the pins

It will be worth it for when I forget I've done it
Opening the door on my hard work
Oh yeah, well done

Life Breath

I enjoy breathing out on everyday objects
Seeing if they move because of me being alive
Candles from a distance
Cobwebs from the bed

That was me
I did that

The longer the breath takes to reach the target
The higher the level of satisfaction
It's more difficult to gauge the impact of my breath when I am
outside
Unless it is cold

That was me I think
Oh
That was the wind

A large gust goes to work on the treetops
Puts me and my breath firmly in my place
Lung capacity feels insignificant in my chest when I see a
newspaper page in the air
I wonder how a spider feels
When it sees my breath move its web

Kicking The Light On Purpose Especially When It's Dark

I go out of my way to kick pavement dwelling still got
something cigarette ends
To lift second-hand sparks from the scrapheap of smoking
Sometimes I take a run up
Impact frees variety and directions
The glow scatters with purpose into finely chopped fire
To make me feel
I got there when I was meant to
For something small on the outside but big on the inside
To do what someone else could have done but didn't
To score in the top corner of what might have been left alone
Interrupting the uninterrupted
And it's over again
I want to explore the discarded to see if there's any life left in it
Going through the bins of people's habits
To prove to myself I can profit from the thrown away

KIWIFRUITS ARE THE EGGS OF BEARS

Ratio Patio

If ratio is ratio
Why can't patio be patio?
I'd love to sit out on a patio
If patio is patio
Ratio should be ratio
Ratio
Ratio
Patio
Patio
Rational
National
Nation

How observational

The You In Younger

I see an increasing amount of people who are younger than me
More than I used to when I was little
I understand that is how age works, but a vicar?
I didn't think I would live to be older than someone who wears
a dog collar
I presume it was a vicar
It could have been a goth who missed a bit

I see a decreasing amount of people who are older than me
Less than I used to when I was little
There is a small group of people with few who are older than
them
If you age to be the oldest person in the world
Do you look around and think

Out of all the people who were alive when I was born
I am the only one who is still living

Do you get to appreciate being the oldest person in the world?
Perhaps it is all interviews and tablets?
The youngest person in the world is a different matter
That is not a title you get to hold for long
A millisecond or two
I look at people as if age is not reverse renovating them too
But I know I am not the only one who time is working on
I've been twenty-one and all the other younger ages
I grew out of them by doing what a living person does

Potential Conversation

Unless somebody listens
We are talking to ourselves
Perfect for those who like the sound of their own voice
You have someone who is listening to you
It is you
Listen to yourself if nobody else will
Even better, talk to yourself and listen to yourself
The perfect combination
For self-exploration
Hello
Hiya
You alright?
Yes
What are you doing?
Same as you
Been busy?
Oh you know
Yes I do
Do you think we should speak to somebody else?
See what they are doing?
Maybe later
What about listening to somebody else?
What will they say?
That depends
That's exciting
Yes it is actually isn't it?
Let's go and speak to somebody and hopefully we will get to
do some listening

Staring Cloud

I'm sure that cloud was there yesterday
I remember looking at the round bits on the left and along the
bottom
Footballs for training kept together in an opaque white
cumulonimbus bag
If it is there tomorrow I am going to have to tell somebody
What would I say?
Who would I say it to?

Hi, excuse me, sorry to bother you
Do you see that cloud up there?
The one that looks like it's got footballs in it?
That cloud was there yesterday
Can you see how still it is?
It's as if it has stopped to look at something
The other clouds are moving as usual
But that one is the person standing still on the pavement
Facing the road
Looking across the street into the camera as people and traffic
rush past in both directions at the same time

They won't believe me
Clouds don't move in both directions at the same time
I will have to tell them to

Look out for it tomorrow
Remember the round bits on the left and along the bottom

If it is gone I can move on
If it is there, staring, what do I do?
How long would it take for people to notice the cloud that
stayed?

Water Evolution

Where did water come from?
Did it evolve from the same place as me?
The sea? Or did it come from outer space?
If there was a big bang was it in anyway wet?
Can something go bang if it is wet? Yes.
Water allows some of my favourite things to live. Killer whales, sharply dressed and shining in their pristine black and white birthday suits. Orange trees, Sir David Attenborough and foxes. I saw a fox drink a whole puddle once. He or she drank the puddle until it was gone and the fox was just there, licking the road where the puddle used to be. Bits of grit in its tongue like a WHAM BAR with small stones for dull zingy bits. The fox looked up at me, as if I had caught it doing something it was ashamed of. I said "hey come on, don't worry, where else are you meant to get yourself a drink from around here? I can't see you turning any outside taps on with those hands, or feet, whatever they are. What are they? Front ones hands? Back ones feet?" The fox just stared at me, like an audience who weren't quite sure yet, and said "PAUSE. I had to drink it, I was looking at my reflection and Mufassa from 'The Lion King' appeared in it. He started trying to tell me that he was my biological father so I licked up the puddle to get rid of him. I'm a fox not a lion. A fox can't have a lion for a dad can it? Sure we all want Mufassa for a dad but we can't all be Simba can we?"
I said "I like you fox, I'm going to give you a name and your name will be Puddles."
Where did foxes come from?
Did their ancestors crawl from the water like I'm told ours did? What was a fox before it was a fox? I want to see the diagram showing the transition from sea creature to furry fox. The half way stage. I'd love to go up to that being and say "you're going to be a fox one day. Well, not you, but you know what I mean?" As humans, we are at the end of the evolution of man diagram, but in years to come I hope we'll be in the middle. Futuristic beings with USB ports for orifices pointing at an illustrated representation of us in disgusted wonder. We can't be the finished product can we? I look around and I think perhaps not.

I feel unfinished, like I've got some serious pieces missing that I could do with. A work in progress. I hope we get to progress. What about rising sea levels?

Don't worry about them Rob. Listen, if the arctic ice melts we can rebuild the arctic from scratch using natural resources and white acrylic paint. Or we could make it from white plastic so it looks like it was made by Apple. Imagine how white that would be, an arctic made by Apple. There's no white like Apple white. But if the world is underwater, we won't be able to ask Siri about the threats of climate change because our phones will be all wet and there won't be any rice to dry our phones in because all the rice will be wet. Wet rice won't fix wet phone, no matter how upright your phone is.

Yeah but Rob, you're forgetting, the rice fields will soak up all the water won't they?

No they won't. This is the only chance we've got. I don't want the people who come after me to have to live their lives like Kevin Costner in 'Water World'. I want them to get to live their lives like Kevin Costner in 'Field of Dreams'.

How about a compromise, Kevin Costner in 'Field of Wet Dreams'? 'Dances with Wet Wolves'? 'The Bodyguard' starring Wetney Houston?

Look Rob, don't worry, someone's working on it somewhere to make it all alright.

Who? Isn't it me? Shouldn't I be doing something? Anything?

Oh calm down Captain Planet. Sir David Attenborough's on the case.

Is he? He can't do it by himself and anyway somebody told me that every time we leave the tap running when we are brushing our teeth Sir David Attenborough gets a dead leg. Out of nowhere. Just when he's walking about. Like some sort of 'It's a Wonderful Life' angel getting its wings bell ringing type deal, but instead of getting his wings he gets a dead leg. I wish I could speak to Sir David because to say the sea is where we came from originally, I don't feel at all at home in there. I am better in water, however, than a shark is out of water. How do sharks feel about water? Probably the same way I feel about air

– ambivalent, until my supply gets cut off. Is a shark better in water than I am on land? I guess it depends on the individual shark. I always think of sharks to be focussed and assertive. They look like they know where they're going and what they're going there for, but I'd like to think there is a shark out there who is the shark version of me. Finds it really difficult to put weight on. Doesn't like swimming after eating. If there is a shark who doesn't like swimming after eating, I feel sorry for that shark. When a shark eats it gets a mouth full of salt water every time it chews. Every meal is seasoned for a shark. No pepper though. Do sharks pray for us to drop a few hundred thousand tonnes of pepper into the sea? So their meals can be properly seasoned? Sharks don't pray, their fins aren't long enough and they don't have anything to get down on. If sharks and other sea creatures found religion and believed their water to be holy water and considered their lives to be some sort of never ending baptism, how would I feel about it? I guess I would be pleased that they have found something to believe in. Octopus in a burqa. I believe in water. I have to. It really exists for me. Especially when I'm washing my hands. It's ridiculous how much faith I have in it. I've got history with water. It runs in my family. Until recently my dad was a plumber. He's retired now. For those who don't know, retired is short for really tired. My dad's dad was a plumber. When I was little water kept a roof over our heads. Gave me a Lego pirate ship for Christmas, a pale green carpet for a Yorkshire ocean. Love infested waters.

Cold weather was burst pipes to my dad.

I remember a knock on the front door one Christmas day afternoon. They didn't know where else to go. Dad went away and then came back and finished off his tea. Sometimes he'd get in, put his clothes straight into the wash, come and find me and say "there's no way you are going to have to do what I have had to do when you grow up."

Telephone Interview With Jobcentre Plus 21/04/09

Does anybody care for you? He asked

No. I replied

Do you care for anybody else? He asked

No. I replied

Wet And Coriander

One event led to another and I was eating coriander in the
shower
We have been growing it in the bathroom
Not in a weird way
In a pot on the windowsill next to the mirror

One morning I noticed a leaf looked big enough to eat
Before I got in the shower
After I'd turned it on but before I got in
I picked the most ready looking leaf
Placed it flat on my tongue
Took my finger and thumb back out of my mouth
It was as if there was nothing there
I knew it had gone in

Pulling the shower curtain across
I put my head under
Biting down on the little there was
I had never eaten in the shower before
I had never eaten coriander when naked before
I guess that's how they ate it in the olden times
Stone Age people and coriander don't go
Coriander must have been around for some of them
Huge unfarmed areas of green
It wasn't invented in the eighties
In the shower the flavour seemed to compliment the water
Maybe some of my cells remembering how simple it used to be
Eating coriander naked in the rain

Slug Volume

I am just pleased slugs aren't loud
Grateful to whoever pointed the remote control of nature at
them and turned the sound off
A noise of constant volume from those individual shiny
cartoon eyebrows would make life more challenging for all
alive and hearing
Keeping us awake at night
With their small-mouthed screaming
Forcing us out in our slippers
Equipped with torch, trowel and bucket
Moving their sound from ground to trowel to bottom of bucket
Collecting the noise
One wet minus at a time
The first slug is a solo artist
Another and the volume doubles
Three and they form 'The Slugs'
After fifteen minutes
The bucket is a heavy wet open top concert hall
Staging a symphony of slime
Those at the bottom fight to be heard
The handle is on vibrate in my hand
Which recycling bin do I put slug noise into?
Garden waste of the imagination

A Face Of My Own

I didn't have a baby face when I was a baby
When I was a baby I had a baby's face
I'm quite amazed that as I grew up my face knew what to do
Skin acclimatised to changes in flesh, muscles, bones and blood
It kept up with me
I'm pleased because I wouldn't want a baby's face on the
middle of my head now
It would be too small
It wouldn't fit me
It would have loads of blank space around it
The man whose face forgot to grow
I wish I could go back in time
I would pull my first visible face again
The one I pulled when I first came out into the world at the
hospital
It wouldn't have been: eyes scrunched up, screaming Munch
mouth
It would have been the face you pull when you are looking
around a flat
Inspecting the walls and ceilings without crying
If only I could have spoken the first time I saw my parent's
faces
I don't know what I would have said, maybe
"Where am I?"
Or
"Who are you?"
Or maybe I would have just said
"Thank you"

I imagine I was crying a lot when I was first born
Was that because I wasn't used to having a face?
Or was I simply not used to being alive?
It was all too new to me
I was all too new to me
The fact that suddenly out of nothing I was something
Something that people could see
I couldn't handle it

Having a face is a lot of responsibility for a person
My face has been with me through everything
The first time I went fishing with my dad
When I rode a bike without stabilisers
When I got bullied at school by a small boy called Ricky
I can see his catchphrase coming from his face now
"MY BROTHERS ARE IN THE NAVY
WHEN THEY GET BACK THEY ARE GOING TO KILL YOU"
I took my face on a school trip to Alton Towers once
We went for a ride on the Nemesis
It loved it
Reminded my cheeks of when I turn a powerful hand dryer up
the wong ray wound and open my mouth
My face was there when I got my GCSE results
When I lost my virginity
When I moved to Newcastle to go to university
When I moved to London to get a job
When I got a job
When I lost that job
When I got another job
When I quit that job
When the police knocked on the old downstairs flat door
They told me my neighbour had been found hanging upstairs
I was instructed not to worry as there were no suspicious
circumstances
That I should make myself a cup of tea
When they left I didn't know what to do
I put my favourite DVD on
'The Flaming Lips Live at Oklahoma City Zoo'
The faces of the crowd
Covered in glitter and wonky costume parts
So much life when death was so near

Usain Bolt's face is the face of Virgin Media
My face is just my face
It is where my life comes out of
It is where other people's lives come into mine

Paper Ball

This is my paper ball
Once upon a time I dropped it onto the pavement
It created a crater
A metre wide and deep
When this happened I climbed into the crater
Held my paper ball up to the passing pedestrians
Exhibited it like a found lost golf ball
They ignored it
I threw this paper ball up to the night sky
It stuck to the black
Like chewing gum when thrown really hard at a chalkboard
that's on the ceiling
It turned the constellations on their heads
Day broke and the ball fell back into my hand
It weighs about the same as a bag of flowers
It is my full stop

Imagining A Memory

Can you imagine how the last few days have been for me?

Well that's all I can do isn't it?
You can remember them
I have to imagine them
Remembering and imagining
These are two very different brain based activities
Imagery conjured up between the compass points of the skull
Why don't you tell me what you can remember from the last
few days and I might be able to imagine the events more
accurately?
The amount of detail you remember will determine how
precisely I imagine they have been for you
Tell me where you were
If I have been there I might be able to remember the location so
I won't have to imagine it
It might have been different when I was there so tell me your
experience of it
Who were you with?
If I have met them I will be able to remember what they look
like and imagine how they will have starred in that particular
situation
I will do this by using my brain
Firstly to remember and secondly to imagine
My heart does not possess these skills
Sometimes when my brain imagines
It forces my heart to believe
My head believes my heart when it comes to belief
What do I prefer? Remembering or imagining?
Remembering is set in the past
Imagining is not tied down by time
I guess it depends where your brain likes spending its life

Umbrella Echo Tango

Umbrella echo tango
Umbrella echo tango

He was saying words into a mobile telephone
Using them
Not for their meaning
Discarding what they stand for

Shelter
Proof you are there
Vibrance in a village hall on a weekday evening

Words are meant for more than their first letter
Umbrella is not a one letter word
It is an eight letter word

Umbrella
Echo
Tango

These are three top flight words
They sound good together
A three piece suit
Umbrella on the outside
Echo on the inside
Tango for the trousers

Growing For Each Other

Did we become the right size for oranges?
Or did oranges become the right size for us?
I am wowed by card tricks as if an apple fitting in my hand
isn't magic
Nature seems tailored
How do the trees know when to stop?
Who told the flowers how to happen?
They can't see their audience yet they perform like that
Conifers, butternut squash, horses
All against making a monstrous scene
What has kept this alive casserole from spoiling
Cat hair is the perfect length for a cat
If it wasn't it would continue to grow
Brushing along the floor
We would have to cut the cat hair
This knocking the confidence of cats
Certain hairs know when they are correct
Like my eyebrows
They are instinctive
Stop
Stay
Cornfields are aware of when enough is enough
Most waves are a perfect fit for a beach
We should be standing in the streets applauding the sun
What was it that got all of this done?
Looking a snail in the full stop eye
With my finger and thumb on its shell
The snail is a familiar size
The snail is life size
I want to be life size
My life size

Solvable

Taking headphones from jacket pocket
I look at the familiar rematch in my hand
I wish someone would invent something
A solution
They would have created it by now if it needed to exist
One player pavement rage on the way to the train
I walk past the performance art
of a man conducting a tight parallel park

You're alright
You're still alright
Stop
You're going to need to go back out again
OK you should be alright at that
Yep yep plenty of room
No

We were struggling to untangle our mornings
One way then the other
This way
That way
Reachable light at the end of our problem tunnels

A System In A System

The closest thing I own to a solar system
Is my digestive system
Complex, dark with twinkling bits I can't see
Just like it is up there
I have seen neither system up close
If I did I don't know if I could take the information in
I can hear my digestive system at work
I cannot hear the labour of the solar system
Maybe I can
Does rain on rhubarb leaves count?
What are the contents of our solar system?
Have a look in the newspaper
The section after the middle but before the sport
I have attempted to digest the Milky Way in my mind
Exploration is difficult when the system is inside of you
As it is when it is outside of you
As a heavy woollen coat is a ploughed fabric field to an ant
To the smallest ingredient of an ingredient
My digestive system is a solar system

From Sighing To Silence

The sound of a stopping hoover
A sigh of relief
A car in a futuristic film coming to a halt
Ears let their guards down once again
Everything settles
Relax
It's over now
The hoover is unplugged
Crumb-free tidy silence
Post hoover volume seems lower than pre
I must have hoovered up some sound
The noise will re-gather
Until the next time I hoover it up
I attempted to hoover the leaves of a plant once
It didn't end well

Q & A & Q

You've got an answer for everything haven't you?

How could I have an answer for everything? I didn't consider everything to be a question until just now. Is everything a question? That radiator? Your shin? If a chimney is a question, what is the answer? Smoke? That's another question. If smoke is a question what is the answer? Fire? That's another question. If everything is a question who gets to ask me? Who is the spokesperson for everything? Many things can't speak to ask me a question so I can't give them an answer. What is the answer to everything?

This is exactly what I'm talking about.

Flame Of An Onion

In the lower core of an onion
I discovered a candle flame shaped flame
How had it not cooked itself from the inside out?
Not wanting to waste anything
I put it in a pan with some butter
I had never cooked a flame before
Jealous blue tongues of heat licked up the pan side

Why does she get to go in there?
It's us down here doing all the hard work
We are hot to heat up food
Not flames from other fire families

I wondered what the flame would taste like
Would it be hot like hot yolk is hot or hot like chilli is hot?
Flames don't taste spicy do they?
It kept its shape and colour quite well
Creating a romantic mood in the pan
For the onions to bid themselves goodbye

NEVER
SIMPLIFY
MOONLIGHT

Gift Shop For The Supermarket

I do my best to look at supermarkets as gift shops
Gift shops selling souvenirs from the world
The employees live in the world and are therefore familiar with
the gifts available
I buy presents for myself
I don't wrap them up because I know what they are
Teams of people have put years of effort into their
development
Bleach
Clingfilm
Oven chips
Deodorant
You may find a small soft giraffe in the gift shop at the zoo
But there are no cuddly boxes of washing powder here
They are the real thing
Strong cornered and functional

Teddies of bags of self-raising flour
Come in the form of actual bags of self-raising flour
With self-raising flour for stuffing and paper for skin
They do not make good teddies
So just buy a bag of self-raising flour as a treat
Put it on your mantelpiece when you get home
To remind yourself of your time on Earth

The Smell Of Jury Service

On the up escalator
A lady two steps in front and above leaves an atmosphere of
perfume
I am moved into it by technology
If this was a diagram from the side
The steps at our feet would be labelled ESCALATOR
An arrow underneath showing us moving diagonally up and
across the page
The fragrance is a cloud from the back of her head to mine
It is a poor diagram
A thought bubble coming from the top of my head has the
words JURY SERVICE written inside
Sometimes, thanks to the perfume in the diagram, situations
reek of the deliberation room
The top deck of a bus
A section of an audience
My nose takes me back to Snaresbrook Crown Court

School dinner tray mentality
Sliding red plastic along four metal bars
The warmth of the lights on my hands

Chips or mash darling?

The word 'calming' must have to feature heavily on your
personal statement to get a job as a dinner lady in a courthouse
You're supposed to be an adult to be on a jury
The dinner ladies return me to child
Nothing like a dinner lady calling you darling to make you feel
like you've got a long way to go
As the perfume moves away like a swarm of bees following a
walking hive

The memories fly back into their brain boxes

Family Tree Of Water

Water
I've had it
You've had it
I look at people in the street and realise they've had it
We've all had it
Every living thing has had it
As human beings we've got to try to have it haven't we?
While we still can
Not only that, but to do our best to allow those who need it
to have it too
This is the only place where we can have it
We can't have it on Mars
It's not there for us to have
If it was
I wouldn't want to move
I want to have it down here
Where I'm part of this
The imperfect water-powered conga of carnage and creation
Great white sharks, astronauts, pot-bellied pigs, nuns and
vicars, bees, chives, kings and queens, footballers on stickers
Water
We are anchored to it
Tarantulas, polar bears, barn owls, bamboo shoots
Seahorses, coconuts, Jersey cows and kiwifruits
Removed family with a thirst for the wet stuff
From the Alsatian to the geranium to the stickleback and back
and back and back and back
The little guinea pig called Patch that I had as a child
Just like Picasso and Elvis and my mum and dad
That guinea pig needed water and to know that is liberating
A truth I can wash myself in
I feel honoured to drink from the same tap as my basil plant
When my basil plant looks like it needs a drink
I give it a drink and it comes back
You know where you stand when something has leaves
You can't water love
Maybe you can

By doing things without being asked
The surprise cups of tea she brings in the morning
I wish you could bottle that feeling of getting a cup of tea from someone you love
Kate Bentley
I take water for granted like I take my lungs for granted
My lungs are in my chest but I very rarely think about them
How is it that the most important can become the most forgettable?
Did I get used to water?
Did I get used to life?
I did but I don't think I ever will
Sometimes it feels like I've been brainwashed into ignoring the chaotic brilliance that has been laid out for me
I want to take my brain out of my head and rinse it under a cold tap to wash away the acceptance of it all
I just hope it doesn't get to the stage where I walk past a fish tank without looking in
Do you wish to continue?
Yes I do

Manifesto

The following words and phrases were lifted from five party political manifestos and put together to create a new manifesto

Our manifesto is based on the simple principle that a
government should be both humane and reliable
You can trust us to put life at the heart of everything we do
Nobody voted to be born
Yet all of us are living with the results of it
As a party, we will promote our robust belief that
There is no such thing as an ordinary person
We are the strong and stable guard dogs for people's dreams
And we must give everyone the opportunity to
Access smooth fairness
You, the many, can trust us to clampdown
on the hope dodging few
Our first urgent task will be to abandon plans to
reinvent the wheel
We will reinvent the point of freedom
We will extend maximum

On day one
We will prioritise the maintaining of rapid access to the future
Through the building of a strong pipeline for hard work
Stretching from ambition to success
It takes courage and determination to set up your own faith
So we will fish in creative waters
To catch the public's imagination

Following the high design standards of nature
We will scrap plans for a new low cost factory built seaside
We will maintain free access to air
Air is the basic building block for breathing space
As a population, we are living together
This is good news
Our party understands that most people don't have time to hate

We will strengthen communities by ensuring
high quality thriving
We will reduce loneliness by delivering
state-of-the-art giant bonfires
Our fundamental belief is that art needs to work harder
but it is still the greatest soft power
We will reverse the cruel decision
for the confident to be bulldozed by fear
And we will focus on our commitment
to create world-class human beings
Furthermore we will introduce legislation to ensure there are
no drops in turbo charged hope

The UK has the world's oldest glorious future
The future is vital
It is the backbone of our tomorrow
But too many of us do not enjoy our billionaires in sport
So we will take action to significantly reduce
the scandalous link between money and winning

We will work to bring in a ban on caged potential
We will cease the love cull, which spreads hate
Health should not be contaminated with arguments
We will fight to make sure that every human gets a
guaranteed number of lifetime hours each week

We will ensure Britain remains a place

TO CUT
A LONG STORY
SHORT-
THE END.